T0288074

IMPROBABLE CREATURES

IMPROBABLE CREATURES

poems by Jon Davis

Off the Grid Press, Boston, Massachusetts

Grid Books
86 Glendower Road
Boston, MA 02131

Off the Grid Press is an imprint of Grid Books.
www.grid-books.org

Copyright © 2017, by Jon Davis. Cover illustration copyright © 2012, 2017 by Grant Hayunga.
Author photograph © 2016, by Jason S. Ordaz. All rights reserved.

Cover painting: Grant Hayunga, "Hare and Raven," 2012, mixed media on paper, 34 x 32 inches, private collection.

Author photograph: Jason S. Ordaz, Institute of American Indian Arts (IAIA), 2016

Printed by Cushing-Malloy, Inc., Ann Arbor, Michigan. Book design by Michael Alpert.

ISBN: 978-1-946830-00-5

ACKNOWLEDGMENTS

I thank the editors of the following journals for publishing these poems:

Crazyhorse: "First Contact"; *Cream City Review:* "The Other Jon Davis" and "The Order of the Goat"; *Diode:* "When the Lights Come On" and "Waterlilies"; *Flash: The International Short-Short Story Magazine:* "The Lovers"; *Miriam's Well:* "Ars Venatica: The Harrier"; *The Moth* (Ireland): "*Babakoto*"; *New Hampshire Review:* "Commencement Address"; *Platte Valley Review:* "Letter of Recommendation for Dave Jonas"; *Ploughshares:* "Early Snowfall"; *Provincetown Arts:* "The Invention of Ecstasy"; *SCREWRENT:* "Sequence: Modal*"; Taos Journal of Poetry & Art:* "Ephemera," "Poetry," and "Epistrophy"; *Terrain:* "Before I Go" and "Empire."

"Ars Venatica: The Harrier" appeared in the *2011 Poetry Calendar* (Bertem, Belgium: Alhambra Press, 2010).
"Early Snowfall" appeared in *Photographers, Writers, and the American Scene: Visions of Passage* (Santa Fe, NM: Arena Editions, 2002).
"Epistrophy" and "Waywardness & Bliss" appeared in *Thelonious Sphere* (Lubbock, TX: Q Ave. Press/Iron Horse, Texas Tech University, TX, 2011).
"October, Los Alamos, 2010" appeared in *Heternonymy: An Anthology*, edited by Chuck Calabreze (Nacogdoches, TX: LaNana Creek Press, Stephen F. Austin University, 2015).
"The Paradigms of Expression" appeared in *West of New England* (Missoula, MT: Merriam Frontier Award/University of Montana, 1983).

With thanks to the Lannan Foundation; the Artists' Retreat at Cill Rialaig, County Kerry, Ireland; and the Institute of American Indian Arts, for the gift of time. Thanks, also, to Greg Glazner, Dana Levin, and Arthur Sze, who try to stop me from making the errors of judgment I persist in making.

This book is for

Teresa, for Grayce and Mike,

for Gregory, Briana, Matthew, and Andrew.

For my granddaughter, Maxine Rael Zayas.

And for the extended and complicated

families I've been lucky to be

a part of.

CONTENTS

You're on Earth. There's no cure for that.

– Samuel Beckett

POETRY

when the tribe lost
       when their supply of ochre
was purchased was stolen
       they rubbed their bodies
with rust from the railroad tracks—
       that the outer world
could visit the inner

ARS VENATICA: THE HARRIER

Wings upswept to stop the endless rising,
spread wide to stall the sudden drop,

he flies nowhere, everywhere at once—
a hollow bird blown up on shafts of wind.

This dance of everything
with feathers and flex, this sensible drift.

This stillness at the core of motion.
Even his call is half query, half wind.

He shuns the shadowed junipers,
startles the reckless vole, hunts

best by pretending not to hunt.
Wafting among the willows, he plies

the seam where wind meets wind.
Wings luffing, curling, buffeted,

they carve an edge almost, but not quite
willed. So when he falls, it seems

just that—a fall. A kite broke loose
he is, blown down half-sideways

in the sage, limp gopher, like
an afterthought, tangled in his claws.

EARLY SNOWFALL

Yesterday's snow falling again
and already. Falling steadily
among vowels, tall consonants.
Alertnesses scumbling among winter cabbages.
The eyebrowed jay named by a man named
for a star. *Stellar's.* When I say the word
the pleasure happens on my palate
and I am never the same person again.
Smoke. Granular. Piñon.
Clouds slumping into valleys.
The idea of snow. The actual idea.
On snow-encrypted branches:
bird-skitter. Then bird.

AGAINST CREATIVITY

They're certain that without it
we'll wince and hobble across
the fire-scorched earth, eyes
shuttered to the finch just
vaulting now from the parapet,
his garbled song repeated un-
changed for centuries. A song
that floats like a nametag
on a conventioneer in February,
when the snow slips from rooftops
and regathers itself beside the half-
buried Toyotas and Subarus,
their iridescent owners haggling
with wipers and scrapers while
the plastics manufacturers lug
their sample cases and pamphlets
conventionward, no stray thoughts
rampaging through their brains,
no innovative patents hovering
like hummingbirds over jonquils
and trumpet vines, slipping
their thin beaks in, their black tongues
laving the bright chalice, the stamen
and pistil, the lovely precise
logic of their devotional—

THE POSTMODERNIST LOOKS AT NATURE

If power is all there is, what then of agency?
The Cooper's hawk leans from the aspen, peers
at the branch still shaking from the finch's quick launch.
It was the shadow of power made the finch flee, driven
not by fear exactly, since fear presumes a concept of time,
but something bred into it by the machinery of survival.
And the hawk is also caught in power's grip,
serving power, lost inside power, a pawn
masquerading as a king. Here where margin and center
blur, before the gendered inequities blossom
into plumage and duty, the nest filled with blue eggs,
the endless setting, this making oneself indiscernible
from the surrounding world, while the males launch
from treetops their flamboyant songs, majestic flights.
Angelic briefly, until deconstructed by light and time
and the excess meaning of *chuck* and *chirr* and *scree*.

FIRST CONTACT

Who are your gods?

Say what a man most is: flesh bringing forth flesh, a dream dreamed by
the ancestors.

Where did you come from?

First the woman dances, then the man lugs the antelope to the fireside.

How long have you lived in this place?

In first light, the boat plying the dark ribbon of the river. The lone
    fisherman, standing, bare-chested, silhouetted. The long pole
    pushed then raised then pushed again. The lean boat, knife
    shaped, carved from the mango tree, slipping silently seaward.

What foods do you eat?

From the black mouths of caves, from the shadows of trees, from mud
    bogs and the dreams of monkeys. Adrift on the warble, the
    insect drone, the *Kyrie* of the red tail.

Tell me about one of your ceremonies?

When the wild dogs encircle the village at night. When the howling
    begins. When the man rises and checks the fence he built of
    sticks and vine. And finds it good. Finds it strong.

How do you heal diseases?

Nothing. Then a thin line where light gives the darkness shape and
    volume. Then high branches festooned with sunlight, the
    glint and dazzle. The waking.

What is your biggest problem?

Full moon on the mountain's flanks.

How do you keep track of time?

The young mother grinds maize. She wears the traditional wrapper,
    sits in the bare dirt, one daughter twirling her hair on her finger.
    The other points to something moving in the treetops.

Who are your leaders?

Eagle on the cliff's edge, big cat on the moonlit plain.

What is the name of the language you speak?

Only the enemies know, and long ago we made a pact not to speak of it.

BABAKOTO

Nothing in my head this morning but that race of humans in
    Madagascar who remained behind in the trees.

The peaceful black and white ones, the *babakoto* who munch leaves and
    greet the day with tremulous keening.

It is said they miss their lives on the ground among their cousins, miss
    the small talk, village life.

I don't recall the details of the story: two brothers, one went to till the
    land, the other stayed in the trees—

nothing about why each chose the life he did. This morning, briefly, just
    before the sun rose,

coyotes yipped and howled close enough to the window that they
    seemed to be calling me to join them.

How dull, this poem, this attempt to make language perform when
    language itself is the beast—

howling inside me, calling me away.

MARRIAGE CAMEL

"This might be the straw
that breaks the marriage camel's back."

Though she might pause & blink like a child
Just awakened in a bright room, she will survey

The flat world & begin again, scuffing and swaying,
Nodding against wind, the silica that lights like ash

On her lashes & ears. Half-asleep but implacable,
She ascends each successive rise with hope,

Then scuffles into the next barren bowl. She
Can do this because she holds an image—

Flute song & dancing, date palms, tents,
Wide pools of water—& is certain that soon

She will crest a dune & enter that festival again,
The festival that quenches a thirst & inaugurates

Another dull plod through sand-blurred blankness,
Tongue dry, hope a fine grit ground against teeth.

SELF PORTRAIT AS ROADRUNNER
AND COYOTE

Stopped and quivered like an arrow thwacked to the bullseye,
but the story unfolded despite them: rock painted black
like a tunnel, cliff edge disguised as a road, explosives planted,
rocket pack strapped to Coyote's back. That one of them
was pursuing the other was the first illusion they had to shed.
When Coyote slammed the rock wall that Roadrunner slipped through,
they began to comprehend. When Coyote leaned to clutch
Roadrunner mid-air. When Coyote fell like an anvil and Roadrunner
beeped and zipped back to safety, they knew this was how it would be—
each of them roaming a different world, their private physics
opening like a rose, like the aperture of a camera,
while the gunpowder flashed—a quick explosion, a woman
and a man kissing in the darkest corner of the night, building a world
out of words, stepping into it, zipping the air closed behind them.

CARTOON FLIP

The cartoon flip, for the beginner, is a cross between doing nothing and a car wreck. I watched Matt awhile because he was watching himself mirrored in the window of my writing room. I'd been trying to write a poem about, after my divorce, meeting with the owners of a one-room guest house in Santa Fe. Teresa had gone with me, sweeping through the house with such lighthearted assurance—praising their color choices, lamenting with them that the cranberry paint had gone purple in the den, that their daughter was shy now, but just wait— that they must have thought I was a man of substance to have attracted such beauty and competence. I must admit that once I got past the sheer wonder of standing beside her, there were days I felt like a man "with prospects," as they might have said of a man in Missouri in 1859 or in a movie, anyway, about a man in Missouri in 1859.

When I moved in a week later, we shifted the bed nearer the heat, moved the pull-out loveseat, and set up a screen so my daughter would have a "room" when she visited. Some nights, Teresa stayed with me, but most nights I was alone with my unfinished poems, stacks of papers, my computer. I held onto her like Ishmael held onto, well, whatever it was that Ishmael held onto. A splinter of wood from a sunken ship? The sunken ship of my life? It made me wonder how the suddenly single—truly single—manage. I was so filled with sadness and wonder that every day seemed both miraculous and fleeting. So when I found the desiccated skeletons of two flickers in her fireplace—the fireplace of the house she was giving up to be with me—I hung them in a tree outside the kitchen as if they were Christmas ornaments.

When my daughter finally came to visit, I don't know how *she* felt, but I was filled with joy. *Bursting with it*, as the saying goes. She wandered the house like a visitor to a museum, flipping open my books, touching the rocks and shells. It was late October, the air clear and crisp, and we walked the arroyo near the house. Someone had left a Frisbee behind, and we began tossing it back and forth. She would run ahead and I would throw it and then I would run ahead and she would throw. We moved up and down the arroyo like that. Just throwing a Frisbee. It was probably some kind of metaphor we were making. First the daughter moves ahead and then the father. Sometimes they catch the Frisbee, sometimes they miss. Each time, if the metaphor is correct, they judge better how far to lead the other. The days are filled with logistics, drives, bills, meals to prepare.

Yesterday, when I should have been loading the Jeep for the landfill, Gregory, Matt, and I stacked the cordwood. I'd planned to stack it conventionally, but I got an idea that we could make a fort. So we did. After a while, Gregory got bored and started pulling out the unstackable juniper logs, twisted and gnarled. "Should we burn this one?" he'd ask, a big smile lighting his face. "Burn it!" I'd say, and he'd say it back to me—"burn it!"—and he'd toss it into the unruly pile, laughing with a glee most of us cannot manage. When the pile of logs got too far from the fort, we formed a line and handed logs from one to the other. Matt was handing me a perfect log, he said—for the top, he said—when he looked up at me. Matthew, the youngest, son of Teresa and her ex-husband. "I love family projects," he said. And even as the clock ticked in the back of my head, I knew that I did, too.

Then Matt was dancing along the line of logs. Then he was back. "It's another perfect log," he said, handing me a slender branch of piñon. And then the fort was complete—four walls, each one taller than

Matthew, because, I told him, a fort's no good if the adults can see into it. And then, because I was the adult, I went outside and checked. I'm sure there's a metaphor here, too. There were places I could stand and just see the top of his head, a swatch of blonde hair, but most places he was safe from my gaze. And maybe that's what childhood is, a place, a time, safe from the adults' gaze. But I was the adult, and so I dropped Grayce's riding boots at the barn, drove back and made Gregory a turkey and salami and pepperoni and provolone and lettuce sandwich and washed the dishes until Matthew called me onto the portal to watch him almost land his cartoon flip.

ON PEAKS

Peaks Island, Maine

Tired of this paradise, the teens
clatter at the gates, drop bikes
on Commercial Street, stay out late
beneath the dock, trading stories—
how they'll get off island soon,
take the boat to Portland and not
come back. By the ice cream shop,
the grade school kids gossip
favorite teachers, field trips they'll take,
call home to beg another hour
in this summer that always feels
like fall. When rains sweep east,
tourists curse, sleep late
to the amplified clatter from the deck.
The locals just nod, a slow day
like any other—only slower. "How long
ya on fawer?" is all they ask,
glad you're here, glad you're going away.
Like drinkers come from a world
too full of drink, islanders choose
not to choose, choose limits, put
Casco Bay, a twenty-minute float
between them and the bustling world.
Most go there every day, come home
to bike-strewn streets, summer folks
who've fled busy lives for humdrum,
go back with almost nothing to report

except they traveled to a world so flat
one visitor spent summer stacking
rocks in six foot pyramids and towers—
elaborate strange sculptures winter
waves will topple, tumble, scatter.

SEQUENCE, JOYCEAN

at Cill Rialaig, County Kerry

I. YES

Clasp and sunder. Glyph and world.
How narrowly in the grass did he.

Severanced by circumstance and a limp,
A dull leg coaxed athwart the bright.

Were he to toss this fetchable stick
And were this good dog to under it run,

Then the world would be joyful a moment,
As when she, unkissable girl, leaned to kiss

In the parked car, him. And began again
The driving heartened, hopeful,

Strange glee warming him though it would not,
Like everything undertaken, end well.

But inside the moment. Despite all he knew
Of futures and failures and misery and cold:

Joy enough. Enough of joy.
Sundered though and limping.

II. MARRIAGE

Lovely it is, but cold, said he.
Can't eat a landscape, said she.

And razed, therefore, the bunkhouse.
And tossed it in the stove.

Hunger much? said he.
Not since the hog died, said she.

Died? said he. Not quite so ineluctable.
Nor so picturesque, said she.

Lovely enough, said he.
If you fancy red, said she.

A pool of it, said he, and thick.
A pudding then, said she.

And a pudding thus they made—

III. JIG

Stauncher in the glove box, they drove
All williwag from the crestview.

Hardly a moment spent in silence
Since the graveward walk begun.

Hardly a day without the rain,
The clouds webbed upon these hills.

Hairs sprouting everywhere, joints
Old hinges squeaking, onion skin

Punctured and bruised. We traded what?
For this wisdom, he wants to know.

Better to be dumb and lovely still, says she.
The world loves *dumb* aright, says he,

And *lovely* while it lasts. It's in, said she,
The beholder's eye. A beholder

Who looks kindly on this, says he,
Is a beholder somewhat further

Toward the grave. And a flatterer, too, says she.
More lie, says he, than flattery, that.

More lie than flattery, that.

IV. THE SHORE

Ghostly in dawnlight. In cold stone. Wind roaring in the glass.
There's cod in the freezer, said he, parsnips in the fridge.

But long since you said anything you meant, said she.
Meant it all, said he. About the cod? said she.

Hardly anything there to hang a coat on.
If by coat you mean a life, said he, then hardly.

Then say, said she, something. There's a wind
Off the harbor, said he. And sheep, said she, in the lane.

Lambing's gone well, said he. Much leaping on wet sod.
If by sod you mean a place to stand and stay, said she, perhaps.

The sheep are certain and strong, said he. Lambs, I can't yet say.
Were it certainty I were after, said she. I'd take a ram.

A ram was good enough once, said he. But I sense
a certain philosophic need. My heart is sore, said she.

Sore or lost? said he. All this rubble and hunger,
All this wind and rain, said she. Lost, then, *and* sore.

'Tis a sturdy house, said he. Of wood and stone constructed.
House for a sore, lost heart, said she. I hear, said he.

Do you now? said she. I do, said he, I do.
Did once, said she. I did, said he, and do.

You mean that? said she. I intend to, said he.
Good enough, said she. Set flame to kindling,

I'll fetch the peat. But your heart? said he.
It's a lonely life, said she. All that water

And hardly any of it gets to touch the shore.

SALISBURY, MARYLAND, 1989

for Grayce

That was the summer of ferries across the inlets,
country fairs, walks among loud birds and flowers.
You were living in a world you'd remember almost nothing of—
not the tilt-a-whirl, the hot dogs, the road
dead-ending at the ferry dock, not the quick drift across
fifty feet of black water, the narrow, humped
roads of the Eastern Shore, not the warblers,
the wren quick in the cattails, its bright bubbling song,
not the house we poked through on Deal Island,
the summer family packing up, not the ants you said
"hello, ants" to every morning. Sometimes, suddenly,
for no good reason, I want that summer back.
Not to do anything different. I'd still lock you
inside the late morning car and have to rush off
to get the extra keys while the neighbor we hardly knew
and never saw again smiled at you from outside.
You'd kick again at the time-out door and when I asked
who was knocking you'd still say "Mi-chael Jack-son."
And every day would tear me up again, walking
with this creature, this daughter, beside me. Small
wispy-haired girl who took each step up to my office,
fearless in pink, or circled and circled
my heat-worn body in the one air-conditioned room
until it was time to flop into my arms and sleep. One afternoon
you flapped and flapped in the backyard, trying
to fly with the birds. For fifteen minutes you ran
back and forth, certain it would happen and why not?

It's twenty years later, but nothing's changed, and you've
still got me thinking this time. This time, if you start
by the magnolia and run flapping towards the board fence,
you'll rise, and when you look down you'll see me
in Salisbury, Maryland, in 1989, looking up, clapping,
running along below you to be there when you finally land.

LAST WORDS: MY FATHER'S

The first last words were my father's.
Late fall, Connecticut, leafless maples,
the sunlight profligate in the neighborhood.
And my father asking me to sit with him
in his beat-up car. He tapped his chest
twice with his fist. *There's something wrong*
inside me, he said. *Be smart,* he said.
Don't be like your old man.
Then the too bright sun.
The silence driving its single spike
between us. And a year later,
the phone, winter then, the drive
to the hospital, and his actual last words—
heaving breaths, as if he were surfacing
from deep underwater. Until he heaved once,
sank, and was lost under the waves, the salt-heavy
green waves churning around us all.

SEQUENCE: MODAL

1. HANDLE

Not the gruesome
Nor the underneath

Petulant then
Strident

Fevered in the dire

Avuncular he was

Uncle Aardvark
Uncle Face in the Window
Uncle You Girls Get Ready

All around us were trees
Green and leering
Wet with grief

Whose vegetables were these
Whose toys

All the touching was a prelude

On the television
The man kept pointing skyward
The woman pounded her heart

Should something
Be done

That was a question

2. BOOK

The book was swollen

Car parked

Shadow under the tree like a cloud of maybe

Like an unspoken agreement

Cats under the porch
Mewling now
Tails in the air now

Rain gossiped
Through an open window

Where is that girl
The house said

Work to be done
The porch said

Kittens around me now

Those battlements

God all over everything
Like grease

Where were we
In the book

3. NEST

Who put all that blue there

Who laced the Snickers in

Hobnailed the lesser

Freed the indentured

Mother's gone to get Jasper

The gold-toothed one

Splayer of the unrighteous

Come here birdies

You call that singing

What God calls a swattable offense

Now you come down from there

Miss Obstructionist

Miss Thinking All the Time

Old one-eyed Jasper

Looking up like a dog on the scent

ON GENRE

But some want to be loved for their rectitude,
others for the depraved precision
of their magic: Look, a hare slipped
through a needle's eye, a goose hid
cleverly between the knuckles
pulled honking from behind the ear.
And isn't the ear another veil, with
its infidelities and amorous nuzzling?
And how is any of this even possible
given the distractions—the fawn wobbling
across the suburban lawn, the flicker
roller-coastering past the statuary.
In the memoir, the beatings were daily,
delivered by a switch clipped
from the backyard hickory. In the novel,
the boy squirmed. His legs were alternately
thrashed, and the welts revealed therefore
an equanimity we could tolerate briefly,
though the denouement would have to explicate
the scars. In the poem, a golden light
fell from the clerestory and the screams
were muffled incrementally by wall
and air and a breeze lifting the branches
outside gently like a mother lifting
her daughter's hair to apprise its gold,
a mother who is really the spirit
of beneficence that visits the world
briefly, like a griefknot or a monkey's fist,

knots almost entirely absent now
from the lexicon. Especially now
that they have dragged genre's net
through the glittering afternoon, leaving
behind a vague amplitude, more wave
than particle, a nutrient, perhaps, more vital
than the hearty meal that has been delivered,
steaming now beneath its silver cloche.

THE PARADIGMS OF EXPRESSION

after Maurice Merleau-Ponty

A rose—
petals velvety as a moth's wings, crimson as papal robes—
droops into fragrant death. These curling parchments
are the documents of love, that brief fierceness
of the affections when we touch
and kiss and create ourselves from dust.

It is raining,
and you, love, are dreaming of betrayal and loss,
a child watching his wagon burn—an impossibility
in a world of impossibilities. The rain falls
stinging the child's face, hissing against the wagon
that burns like acetylene, like metal consuming metal,
and then, inexplicably, a heron in the sky
as if to say, *this is only a dream.*

It is fine,
this praise of loss—the rose wilting,
the impossible wagon impossibly burning,
the child's grief for his lost world. These
are the paradigms of expression, longing
and love and the love of longing. These
are the lessons of language:

man is mortal,
and the parched body leads us into speech
where everything we need enters

and is stilled: the rose, the rain and the wagon,
the heron and the history of flight—
there, and *there*, and *there*.

EPHEMERA

They emerged through layers of blackness and cold.
Hatched out, they uncurled and began swimming
toward this new world of light and wind. They
broke the surface and heard the humming, surprised to be
among so many like themselves. When their wings dried,

they spread them, like cellophane, and rose,
miraculously, and flew. Then the sunlight blasted
everything—the spiderwebs above the stream,
the golden spiders, the stream itself, the speckled
backs of trout where they lay like dreams

one cannot quite remember. The water, when it splashed,
caught the light, then let it go so it could go on
cherishing the moss-edged river rocks, the undersides
of aspen leaves, the fisherman's hair,
lifted now in the breeze. Poorly made for this life,

they dizzied upward into the dangers. Drawn
but no one knew why. Then spent hours touching
the water lightly and launching off again or muddling
in the shallows, half-drowned, half-pasted to the surface
with a million others like themselves. Finally

they realized their one task, a kind of art: to make
more like them who would unburden themselves
of darkness and launch briefly into dazzling sunlight.

And when they understood, in the moment
they understood, they started falling

through layers of blackness and cold and were gone.

IMPERIALISM: AN INTRODUCTION

First they killed the Comanche, then they let the cattle out.

So comfortable they were, their noses in the matted grasses.

Grown thick with muscle, they were paraded to the abattoir.

The architecture, until Donald Judd arrived, was utilitarian.

Trees were scarce, so they built with blocks and bricks and mortar.

It was their habit to grow a small grove to break the wind.

But this made it easy for the Indians to find them.

Thus the philosophic traditions were primarily existential.

Wittgenstein, it is said, passed over Marfa in silence.

But the town was named for a character in a Russian novel.

The train tracks recall Karenina, but the water tower

Is more Woody Guthrie, whose brand of socialism

Was not welcomed here. At least not until the New Yorkers

Showed up with their rattlesnake boots and Americana music,

Their bandanas and banana daiquiris. The cast of imperialism

Still haunts every gesture, every windblown garment.

WRECK

When the night when the firstlight crisped—

When the complete thought arrived with its hooks and lances—

We were surmounting the dream accomplishing heights, et cetera—

From there we would encumber the landscape—

Enormity had pockets and inside the pockets a plaintive darkness—

In there we would crumple in there we would sob—

For the glittering crushed metal for the quick spark and explosion—

Bursting and flaming and redding the dark—

All stream and billow all blackness roiling all edged with flame—

Blown back though we were not present aflame though we did not see—

This life so brief and then—

WAYWARDNESS & BLISS

If from still water stillness rose.

Earth rolling under stars.

Recrudescent, those stars. Hinged.

Hinged as a door is hinged.

A trap door.

Inside: waywardness & bliss.

The streaming. The voices of.

Swept away.

Those whose longings were cured by other longings.

Those who had rolled their pantlegs & waded in.

Those who'd held the child's hand & waded in.

Had stood a moment in the gulf of longings.

Waves swelling against the pilings.

First longing, then wistfulness.

Then silvery fish, quick in the shallows.

Unhinged, those stars.

Wishes all over them like ants on jam.

CASUAL POEM

This casual poem is just
pretending, hiding the bee-stung
darkness in its chest
like a just drawn-in lungful of smoke.

It wants to say *all is well,*
that the gathering clouds are
just clouds and not some menacing
metaphor for the future.

It wants to lean back and close its soft
brown eyes and dream itself
onto a tropical beach
some cruise ship's mendacious occupants

are about to spread across
with their bags full of lotions
and shades and umbrellas,
earbuds and miraculous new beverages.

Did the poem say *mendacious*? It meant
salacious, though most are past
the ability to act on their whimsical fantasies
about this or that body and how they might

fit together, what feverish sensations
these new attentions might induce in this or
that tanned and recently zumba-ed, body.
But the erotics of this are all wrong,

the poem says, gazing now
at the horizon, where all things end
or begin depending upon our
current relationships here

on this side of everything
that's already happened. But maybe,
the poem wants to say, there's hope
for you, for her, for these straw-hatted

multitudes, the likes of which
keep spewing forth from the hold,
certain that some sun, a few waves
gentling the line of pebbles

they keep sifting through
is a meaningful ritual
like a woman in her jewelry case—
which pair of earrings? Which bracelets?

Which bangles, which glittering
to brighten this life,
this day, this beginning
again again again?

BEFORE I GO

I want to say the guacamole was pleasant,
metallic and viscous, and the ornamentation,
while excessive, contributed a certain vagueness
to the otherwise overly-managed event. For instance,
the various proposals concerning the movement
of shoulders and hips, the recent prohibition
of leaning-beside-the-punch-bowl, the manic outbursts
of praise near the X-mas tree. For that matter,
the damaging claims made by carolers, the rigid order
for the revelation of gifts, the marked lack of scholarship
concerning holiday rituals, the call for more endnotes,
the codified nutmeg ritual that lost all spontaneity
with the addition of fiber masks and surgical gloves,
though our hostess's eyes flashed dramatically
after the sanitary draping of nose and mouth.
The gifts, while paltry and too hastily wrapped,
were a welcome addition to the festivities.

I want to say your ardor, however manufactured,
was appreciated. I want to say I will place this lovely
figurine in a place of honor. Did I mention
the fervor, the panicked caterwauling in the coat room?
The vestments lifted, each in their turn, and displayed
briefly like unwanted kittens discovered
in the back hall closet. The squalling, the convulsive
laughter, the demeaning appraisals were, it's true,
uncalled for, but the garments were—how to
characterize them? For amongst the dull tweeds

and camel hairs were the sudden flights
of "wearable art," the cheery pastels,
the loopings and frayings—these were the cries
of those grown brazen with death's approach,
certain that something needed expressing
though uncertain what it was and who
it might be that would do the expressing.
If our endorsements seem overly energetic,
if our enthusiasms trend to the mawkish,
know that we are credentialed by these garments,
sponsored by the darkness leaning its black fur
against the windows. Every departure is fraught,
each leave-taking tragic, now that the snow has begun,
lovely in its erasures, its glittering whiteness
a miracle, so coherent and so meaningless.

THE FUTURE OF MUSIC

after Matthea Harvey

Few among the fastidious would mistake
this mordant furor for a gamelan. Still, the galoshes
abandoned outside the door should clue you in:
gangrene, gaslight, grown men hopping
through the hopeless galley of instruments.
The engineer, haughty among the sliders.
The infinite slipping into the equations now,
consanguineous now, an irritation
in the cosine, an unforeseen irruption.
Jury-rigged construction of gong and jampot,
the jilted guitarist kissed during karaoke,
now limp in lamplight, lachrymose
on the midnight lawn. The moon mentioned
in line three mandated a mawkish intro,
a nacreous nattering, a net of nerves
before the return to normal, or what passes
for normal here in the near future
where we negate our misfortunes
with manic narcotics, mechanical missives.

WHEN THE POET DRINKS VODKA

She lifts the bottle and stares at the medallions
and oryx, antique fonts and frosted glass —

Rooks launch from iced-over branches,

the fields fallow now —

whatever those weeds once were
are a tangle of tunnels for voles and ermine now —

Quickly for the borders are closing —

Quickly for the communist automobiles are purring toward the checkpoint —

Quickly for the rooks are carving a slow arc across the gray mountains —

And the snow is flashing
and swirling as the border guard leans in —

She has no clear identification —
Her ancestry a liability here —

But the liquid is clear the taste like an icicle
hung seasoning from a hemlock —

And the rattle of ice cubes is like the sound —

In the mind's "delicatest ear" —

of words rustling in their dens,
scuffling upward —

into the light into the poem —

OCTOBER, LOS ALAMOS, 2010

after Arthur Sze

In the rose garden, I find yellow chanterelles,
sense a syzygy in the arrangement of fungus, rose, hawk.

You may find teeth marks in late season apples or throw
I Ching in a stone courtyard at dawn. The first notes

of the changing season sound in aspen leaf, salt cedar.
As one watches a mime press hands to imagined glass,

feel long hours of practice like wind at his back.
I peel back a pomegranate's leathery skin, touch

moist red seeds of memory; a Seminole elder
poles through saw grass; an arctic tern arrows

into a fulminating ocean; I hear the *click click*
of a saxophone's keys, creak of piano pedals

and think of the incidental music of wind
across an opened door. I watch you lean

to the winter rose, one hand cupped at its side
as if to touch a child's bruised cheek. Are memories, too,

swept away at infinite speed when a dying star collapses?

THE NOVELIST'S WIFE

It was snowing in Missoula. The baby, who had been fussing in the midst of her teething, was finally asleep. When the novelist's wife looked out the second-floor apartment window, she could see Higgins Avenue, but only vaguely—the buildings across the street had what she wanted to call "an impressionistic cast." It was the kind of phrase she heard when she went to the parties the writers held after their readings. Her husband, the university's visiting writer this semester, was across town, holed up in a little-used room in Jeannette Rankin Hall. Rankin, she knew, had been the only senator to vote against the United States entering the two World Wars. The building named for her was gradually falling into a kind of comfortable disrepair. The grad students who had offices there actually liked its worn surfaces, its rickety furnishings. Her husband was working on his novel—first by hand in the quiet privacy of what he had begun calling "The Abandoned Room," then, later, on a computer that he worked on by arrangement with the secretary down the hall. She'd seen the secretary. She had an odd name—Giselle or Jacinth, she couldn't exactly remember—but she did remember the shy, pretty way she had of brushing her hair back and holding it away from her face when she talked. She seemed like a woman from a poem by one of the Romantics—a little *wan*, she wanted to say, though she wasn't sure exactly what that word meant. Remembering the secretary was what had made her forget the novel in her lap and gaze east, in the direction of campus, into the falling snow—the small flakes that angled earthward, only to be blown upward in sudden violent swirls as they neared the street. She took several deep breaths, trying to calm herself. Her husband would be home soon. She would see the six o'clock bus turn onto Higgins, moving slowly through the dusk-light. The buses are still running, she thought. Soon, her husband would step off onto the sidewalk below—briefcase in hand, brim of his baseball cap pulled low to protect his eyes. He'd check his watch, unzip his jacket, run his hand along the buttons of his shirt, straighten his belt. Then he would rummage through his pockets for the keys, becoming almost invisible in the swirling snow and shadows beneath her window.

EPISTROPHY

who gave us the drop-legged stride
twirled in airports
wore jeweler's glasses & the flamboyant hat
who muttered & slammed
said *ain't no wrong notes on the piano*
dashed to the keys bristling & snapping

then the long silence
the unencumbered
unrippling keys:

                    lake at dawn
                    owl's flight
                    empty boulevard

turning in quarters
he in quarters turning
step & thrust
the tapdancer's flourish

you can see it:

                    listening is almost enough
                    almost enough almost

enough then
it's
suddenly

        not

THE INVENTION OF ECSTASY

after a sculpture by Susan Lyman

"People Look Ridiculous When They're in Ecstasy" is the name for a group of branches and vines grappling or made to seem as if grappling. Is the name for a sculpture I have never seen. But I've imagined the crooks and corkscrews, the conjunctions and appeasements, the whole abstracted mess of longings / longings satisfied / new longings arising, the thin, sharp-edged shadows, the polished look of branch and vine stripped bare and lacquered, the impossibility of single-mindedness, of coordination, control, the wildness tamed—but not quite—and the new wildness Susan put there. Yes, people look ridiculous in ecstasy. *Ecstasy:* "standing outside." As in Eliot's "third who walks always beside" or those Antarctic explorers who, in the extremity of their need, "had the constant delusion that there was *one more member* than could actually be counted." But to be *in* ecstasy, to be *in* that outsideness. And the other case—to be *outside* ecstasy, to be forever outside. What sadness rises in the eyes. An abject emptiness that invites ridicule. But not that other ridicule. Not that envy, that longing to forget one's body, the pain residing there, the appointments and dislocations, the cat that is the heart pacing and clawing the furniture, demanding to be fed. Not the ridicule arising from that, but from this: From the straightness of these vines and branches, which are brittle but not yet sad, are funny, though, are *ridiculous.* So we stand around in our tight shoes, in our bodies heavy with pain. We take out a cable and cinch the tree trunk. We nail the vine to the branch, the branch to the wall. We carve our initials, strip the bark. "Here is the apple with the razor inside," we say. "Here is the poisoned meat." We point, we laugh, we jostle each other and dance. We unwrap these gifts. We giggle and guffaw. "Welcome," we say, and we slap our knees, "welcome to the invention of ecstasy."

THE LOVERS

They were smoking forty feet from the entrances to public buildings. They were coughing into their sleeves, washing their hands before returning to work. They were limiting their intake of saturated fats, disposing of items in the proper receptacles. They were checking their pulses at regular intervals, crossing only at corners. They were wearing sturdy shoes, stopping occasionally to catch their breath. They were hydrating, practicing safe sex. They were coming to a full stop before turning right on red. They understood that their speed was currently 45 40 35 30. They were using the lanes for loading and unloading only. They were refraining from smoking while walking throughout the airport. They were maintaining control of their luggage at all times. They were folding their boarding passes so that the bar code was face up. They were turning off and stowing all electronic items. They were waiting patiently for the captain to turn off the fasten seatbelt sign. Though they were free to roam the cabin, they kept their seatbelts tightly fastened while they were seated. They were neither smoking, nor disabling the smoke detectors. They were placing their smaller items under the seat in front of them. They were returning their seatbacks and tray tables to their full upright and locked positions. They were not anticipating a loss of cabin pressure. They were placing the oxygen masks on their own faces first, then placing the masks on the faces of their loved ones. They were breathing normally.

WHEN THE LIGHTS COME ON

New York City, Winter, 2011

Not the nascent clatter, though that's welcome. Not the flag raised against darkness. Not the tawny cabs purring curbside. Not the snow piled in the square, though its fulsomeness weans the city from night. Not the flat blue above tendriled elms, string of lights, sudden bricks and glass, blurred taillights, exhaust-haze, lone woman on a bench, lampposts leaned like swans over the causeway. Not the boulevard's constellations forming and shifting, conspiracy of lights glowing in offices. Not the entire quickening, but this: a man looks out, past the fire escape's wrought iron and feels—in dusky light, before the day succumbs to rumble and hum, to clatter—a tender hopefulness, like a boy shooting baskets in an empty gym who thinks every dream still possible, every shot going in.

LAST WORDS: THE BRIGHTENING

I liked best the way the sun blanched the horizon,
the way tree branches against that light complicated things,
the hard edges of houses, a window lit up,
a man rising, pulling on his thin robe,
slipping out to heat water, listening to the news,
the great wheel of history slowing, the creaking inside—
all the way down where the bearings were tightening—
the coffee brewing, the man scuffling to the bedside,
waking his wife with a light kiss, while outside—
the brightening, the last owl's faint hooting.

SEQUENCE: THE LIGHT IN TULUM

I. NEAR COBA

Hard by the highway, the spider-legged girl
pedals, jittery as a butterfly in wind.
The dreamcatchers, spinning in the breeze
the traffic wakes, are big enough to catch

a whole town's dreams, big enough
to spin the spider-legged girl across
two lanes of tourist cars & winding taxis,
so jittery we hardly notice her *abuela,*

hawking burritos beside the speed bump—the hard
jolt, her voice calling *dos por uno*
in the span between brake & clutch & gas again,
between the whole & the rent,

the rented breath we breathe,
the heart clutch, spasm,
the jolt the spider-legged girl
just cruises past, wobbling now, oblivious.

II. IN TULUM

In graves they dig at shoreline
workers bury the flotsam kelp.
They heap & tamp, while
kite surfers rise above the waves

like the dead rising incorruptible.
The water heaps then rolls & breaks,
sliding toward the flotsam sunbathers.
The gravid roar sounds deep

inside their chests, deepening
the call of water to rolling water,
like breaking waves of memories
that rise, & rising, crash harder

on the risible sand, until just
one clear wave of *now*
& *now again* rolls out—a noise even
the ear believes is sounding from inside.

III. NAUTILUS

The chambered nautilus,
a cathedral of pearl & suture,
brightens even the darkest room—
wave on wave breaking against

the terrible breakage, room
opening on room, labyrinthine
pearly light of some heaven, some
chambered moonlight gleaming walls,

so we who are walled by fear are made
heavenly by inwardness, the door
that suddenly opens—if the Buddha
is correct—on this ordinary breakage.

IV. THE LIGHT IN TULUM

What's hidden here
beneath the stratigraphy
of clouds, the *isolato*
of the undertow,

are the underfed,
that isolate flock
in the stratified village
(the *barrio* hereafter

of torchlight & *afters)*—
its strategies of rage.
This village—made
classless now, mysterious.

Only mystery, said Lorca,
makes us live—village
of genuflection, rage, village
of altar, wafer, white white light.

V. CANCUN

The waves in Cancun break from blue to brown,
pitch surfers in a pandemonium of froth.
Pelicans glide wing tip to water.
The distance glitters in sunlight or darkens

under clouds. The glitterati dress for tea,
tip lightly, clutch designer scarves.
Pitched deathward, they give skin to salt, to wind,
turn brown & browner on this spit of sand.

Browning, Frost, turned song to story; Stevens
turned it back to song. Death is mother
of both beauty & design. Under clouds,
the glitterati sink, or seem to, into sand.

WATERLILIES

Monet's waterlily paintings are full of the dead: The heaped corpses, the browns and grays, the scarlet mouths of flowers. And Renoir's boating party continues its ferocious dedication to decorum and flirtation. We'd do anything to forget the bloated bodies flowering on the cratered battlefields, or heaped in the trenches, the steady deathward plod, clods of marl and shattered limbs, men blinded by powder, guts splayed, the beautiful ruin. "O, o, o," she says, "mon petit chien." Later they will dress the poodle in ribbons and feed her biscuits. Later, they will step along the marshy shore, dainty beneath their twirling parasols. When the lady's shoe stabs the mud and is sucked from her foot, they will open their red mouths and cry out. "She was leaning to see the lilies," someone will say to the man who glides lightly over the spongy earth to where she stands, one foot lifted, her leg like the neck of a swan startled from grazing, ready to flatten herself along the grass and hiss.

DEAREST M

1.

If you will tell me your new name, I will tell you mine. I could be Randall Bane, though I worry its closeness to *banal*. I knew a poet who changed her name to Lettie Hank. Her poems became lyrics for shape-note singing in a wind-infused West Virginia cabin overlooking the lopped-off mountaintops once larded with coal. One must have a mind of winter, que no? Whatever our names turn out to be, we should study the ecstatics regardless. Mallarmé. The Spanish mystics. The Chileans. The unmoored Moors. The abyss-gazers and pressers-at-the-gates-of-dream. Lost poets lowing in the well. There is a wall between who we think we are and who we are. The mundane is only a disguise the miraculous wears, a dull suit to make it through the day.

2.

Midnight. The event tonight was splendid, though the fireworks and brass brand were probably a miscalculation. Still the white half-boots of the drum major were dazzling in the spotlights. Kicked so high and the pinkish calf exposed. When we dream of hummingbirds, the gates of desire open. Then the rush and lather. Your earnestness a squall in an otherwise calm sea. A bruised apple on the sill. Someone singing "Jesus Is On the Mainline" in a darkened room. One towel. A heart etched on the steamed-over mirror. Water. Tile. An assault that sounds like a thousand kisses. Assault? I meant assent. The sailors drunken and caterwauling as the ship moved through the locks. All the boats lifted and still you don't call.

3.

When the waltz ended, every dog howled. The peasant in the darkest corner gnawed the last bit of gristle from the femur. I thought of you when the trombonist honked his flurry of notes to end it. The song. The night. A flagon of ale and a slow retreat. How ardent you were! You pored over the text as if the fading letters were a thin gruel, were the slick noodles of meaning in a meaningless stew. You think I am lucid when I should be pellucid. Opaque when I should be coughing softly into my fist. In the language of God—a kind of furry Latin. Brush it one way, it glistens. The other, light curls around and around in it like a dog. Then sleeps. Meet me on the other side of the river. The stentorious one. The duck-flecked one. The river that divides mundane from mystery. I sleep beside those waters.

COMMENCEMENT ADDRESS

However…
—Professor Irwin Corey

It is a great & misbegotten pleasure
to be wilting here among you,
the sandwashed sons & daughters
of the recently merged, here
in the torpor, in the kindled rash
of August, along the sand-raddled
banks of the Gitahoolie, that nameless,
time-encrusted squiggle
on the overburdened maps.
Where the stickleback curls
in its bubble nest. Where the lammergeier
cribs a knockwurst from the bagelman.
Where the bagelman creeps along the focaccia
like a budgerigar on fire. Let me begin
with a brief synopsis of the challenge
that lies ahead for you, the Institute's
neotonous & yet gravid class of 2000.
First, there is the Formica of the Lost,
little-explored, but formidable
nonetheless. Then, in rapid
succession: The Festival of Poor Reception;
the tangled sweathog by the macramé;
the callous preacher in the bean dip; the grifter
with the head of a calabash. And
the hoarse admonishments: You call this
an airline. You call this a fortuitous

Afghani. The dreamers have whelped
the bailiwick. They've catapulted the melons.
They've capitulated by the squeezebox.
Ladies & gentlemen, here
are your craven muskox. Here are your
cantilevered hooligans. All this, my children—
the cartoon vixens, the crenelated wombats,
the swarthy G-Men & their pathogenic
G-wives—all this, my children—
from here to the dimpled horizon, from
here to the quadruple bypass, from the crapulent
to the untested, from the fortuitous masqueraders
to the fortitudes masquerading
as vipers—all this, my children, will someday—
bring the knockwurst! bring the jalapeño dip!—
will someday—hail the Coptic savants!—be yours.
Thank you my synthesized drummers, thank
you my husky *baby, babies*. And thank you
my extrinsic cadavers, my mutton cravers, my
greedy unwashed, my halfwit Carpathian sidekicks.
Today is an important day in your lives,
in your parents' lives, in the lives of your countries.
Today is a grievous finicula, a cavernous
sinkhole, an encrypted fiction. Today, well,
we all know what today is. It is, of course,
a severed hand on the chifferobe, a slandered
politician weeping in the vestibule. We all know,
each of us, what today truly is:
a flatulent gaucho, a convex
caravan, a fortuitous affliction,

a sweat-drenched Caravaggio, a garrisoned
battalion of lunchboxes. Thank you
for this opportunity to thwart
your earnest hopes. Go forth then
with your magisterial airs,
with your bloody slipknots. Go forth
then, newly inducted into the splendor.
Go forth benighted ones. I think
I speak for everyone here—your impoverished
benefactors, your goat-bearded
mentors, your avid creditors.
We already anticipate
the gnarled vexations, the avarice
and spleen of your defibrillated careers.

LETTER OF RECOMMENDATION
FOR DAVE JONAS

Never pay a poet by the hour.
—Chuck Calabreze

Although I do not know Dave Jonas well, I have seen him lying awake at night, his griefs and regrets upon him like spiders. I have seen the webs they spin, the way he tears at them with the very hands that shaped his past into an irrevocable chaos that even now looks like the absence of light at the bottom of a bottomless lake. And yet I recommend him highly to your program with its rotting railroad ties and slapdash, though often critically praised, settlements in the heretofore uninhabited zones. Mr. Jonas might be a welcome addition, carrying, as he often does, a bundle of pickaxes, spades, and shovels on his back. Unlike many of my colleagues, Mr. Jonas has not settled into a comfortable mediocrity; *his* mediocrity has been hard won. He had to tear himself from the grasp of a brilliant future, lock himself away, stuff every gap with old, worn T-shirts, avert his eyes to avoid the descent into success. But avoid it he has, with the assistance of a panoply of bad habits and misprisions. His work is consistently late and often incomplete. His signature is a searing genius boggled by vicissitude and ambivalence. And just when one might expect some extraordinary insight, one is met with a tepid image, a trailing off, a frustrating incompleteness, an image, say, of a mouse nibbling a cracker quietly in a midnight kitchen, or of a toaster oven, not cleaned for months, bursting suddenly into flame. The trepidation with which I tender this letter can be traced to this: Were Mr. Jonas to depart, the performance of those remaining might be held to a higher, more universal standard that would place all of us in jeopardy. If I can be of further assistance in your evaluation of Dave Jonas, please let me know soon: What little I believe I know of him is under constant threat of revision.

SELF PORTRAIT AS MOCKINGBIRD

What is this mockingbird, lascivious and bold,
launching its bright concatenations in the shrubbery?
And what dulcimer is the dawn that it should be
so struck? Fact of sun. Of reddening cusp,
a cupidity requiring this arch redress. This mellifluous
apology to night. Songless night. Night of jostling
and dreams. Night of fears and deaths, of endings
and vacancy and loss. But now the mockingbird
has decided to publish an anthology of birdsong,
volleying from the neighbor's chimney: phoebe,
titmouse, starling, finch. His talent to be everything
at once. Great novelist in the dawn, he'll fade
to one-hit wonder by noon, singing this summer's
vapid top-down hit over and over, suddenly timid
in the low brush, the white flash in wings and tail—
last evidence of this dawn's flamboyant run.

THE MAN IN THE COFFEE SHOP WINDOW

That he stares at the November trees. Not the boles, but the limbs etched on a cloud-fraught sky. That he thinks such a sky might be reasonably described as *fraught*. That his reading glasses ride his nose like books on a teenaged girl's head. A girl who has read the book on her head, the book that encourages her to place a book on her head. That he seems to have lost his way, if *lost* and *way* can be brought to bear on someone who cultivates lostness, encourages it, waves it in through the door like a cold breeze. An inevitable breeze and yet he waves it in. Can't wait. The library is closed to celebrate the warriors, and he cannot decide how to feel about that. Each warrior seems reasonable enough, but gathered together into an army? Couldn't they have foreseen the consequences? They have lined up along the crest of the hill and what's left to do but the charging, the plunging, the weapons launched and fired, the falling and writhing, the limping, an energetic music pushing them along like a strong current? Like a current of words. This current. And currently, the man in the coffee shop window is arranging and rearranging a newspaper, his laptop, reading glasses, coffee cup. Inside him, a small, thin man is stretching his legs, removing his shoes, wiggling his toes. Inside him, a lost boy is going from adult to adult in a dark flood of slacks and skirts, peering up at unrecognizable faces. Fear is a trapped bird in his chest, wings beating at his ribs. He believes he has something to say about the warriors, the closed library, the fraught sky, but the lost child is looking up at him now, saying, *Who are you? Why did you leave me? Once they said smile big and gave me a silver coin and now I cannot stop.*

SELF PORTRAIT AS THE COMMUNIST MANIFESTO

I had already arrived by the time I arrived. With my broad shoulders, paunch, penchant for darkness, the painful trajectory of working conditions since feudalism. Paper-thin and yet they feared me. I rose up singing solidarity, singing switchblade in the back, singing my time will come. Inevitable as death, I waited in the alleys, hunched under a cardboard roof while it rained for two centuries. When my opening lines finally arrived, someone hurried the words into print and thus began the decades of interpretation. What had I said, really? Some said *death to the bourgeoisie.* Some said *brutal dictator.* Some said *lovely the flowers and dancing in sunlight.* Murderous enigma: when my author died penniless, they built a bronze statue his ragged disciples could visit, just as they visited my rigid texts, the failed vituperations, the dream of plenty, while the pigeon dragged one gnarled wing along the sidewalk, its pained *coos* bouncing off brownstone and bronze.

THE ORDER OF THE GOAT

Begin with a vortex, anodyne and grave. Apocalypse of bleats, blur of vexations. Add a waiter. A provisioner of meats, hawker of sides, slosher in the tidal rush. Then let the chef decide, for she will decree unkempt salads, olives warm as tongues, dapper oysters adrift in their ragged boats, pork bellies, baby octopi, escargot ravioli like letters from a secret lover. Then she will initiate the Order of the Goat. It will settle tableward serenely amidst the ruckus and folderol. It will induct and beknight. It will command an audience, commend itself thusly: It will shred easily to the tendered fork, make even vegetarians dream of rocky hillsides, the steep ascent. Orbited by minions and by minions consumed. A brief for friendship, a prolegomena for poetry, this conspiracy near midnight, this vaunting of the heretofore unvaunted, this cataleptic and tenderest night.

THE OTHER JON DAVIS

Fissured and skewed, he was. Occasionally mellifluous. His idea of a vacation: to climb a tree and shout at the neighbors. Such were his settings, always tilted toward excess, always heating the floors so that we could not properly walk without asbestos slippers. They tried to peel the layers back but found only more layers. When he stooped to retrieve his cast-off jottings his head glowed white like phosphorous or the sun on a gray day. Nobody knew where the otherness came from. It was thought to involve calcium, magnesium, some uncorrectable imbalance. We tried every conceivable adjustment yet a certain vagueness kept creeping into the equations. See where this vector intersects this wave, the phenomenologist said. But it was no use: one Jon Davis gesticulating beside the kiosk, the other holding a garden hose, dampening the chrysanthemums.

THE DANCING

This unfamiliar planet. Strange trees,
a clearing. Yellow and black birds calling
from the undergrowth. A sun that circles low
on the horizon and never seems to set.
Your tribespeople have gathered around you.
You are dying, they say, but on this planet,
dying is a long, slow process. Especially for one
as important as you. Apparently, you were
in charge of something and questions
have been raised about the discharge
of your responsibilities. But nobody
says a word. Each tribesperson with a complaint
comes forward to *dance* their frustration.
They wear bells on their ankles and wrists.
They shake rattles made of shells. A hood
or a veil covers their faces. At first,
it makes it easier not to see their eyes.

You seem to have lived on this planet
your entire life, but you still don't understand
the customs. These are your people,
but you don't know how to speak to them,
so you sit in the appointed chair, a throne
made of spruce branches lashed with vines,
and you watch: the woman in black, red feathers
tied to her arms. She dances an angry dance.
Or it seems angry; it could be sad or bereft.

When she finishes, she simply stops, turns,
and walks in silence back into the crowd.

Then the man begins. He's old and his stomach
jiggles when he dances, but the effect is not comic.
He lifts his feet, each time as if
for the last time. He's weary, and you seem
to recall contributing somehow
to his weariness. You made him chase you
through the village? Made him want to kill you?

Next up, a woman who will outlive you
by many years. Her veil is red. Black bands
of leather are cinched around her arms.
She dances like a horse rearing to stomp
a rattlesnake. She is fear first, then vengeful rage.
Ah. You remember this one—and your task.
You begin to sob. It is too late to undo
the damage. As each dancer approaches,
you know, you know, you know, you know.
On this planet, this fragile planet, which is every
planet: The dancing will continue forever.
You want to see the eyes. The eyes can lead
to forgiveness. You will not be given the eyes.

COUPLE, SLEEPING

after Lucien Freud

Greyed by light and age, flesh falls away from bone, pools at their bellies. His arm around her is an unopenable gate, rusted at the hinges. Her closed eyes flutter under the lids. She is a particle in a field of thinking. An aching in the wash. His spine, a twisted vine. What little we know of them: a paperback splayed on the nightstand; dentures floating in a glass. The scene is lit by cold morning sunlight. That we are not yet them makes it possible to look. The beauty, if it can be called that, lies in the managing of surfaces, depths, the way shadows pull at the angled flesh. Not the despair ticking inside. Not fear stiffening the arm. But the ash fallen over them. The way time has worn them. Skin tenting the gullied flesh. Batlike, they sleep through morning, his arm now gentling her awake in the risen sunlight.

LAST WORDS: SUCH SIMPLE CREATURES

We were such simple creatures really, wanting, and wanting to be wanted, the legless woman laughing in her chair at the market, the model turning to thank the pilot, walking into the blades of the propeller, the man speaking through the hole in his throat, something pulling us through our days, another sunrise calling us, though everything says *sleep*, though everything says *no*, but then it's summer and Santa Fe and someone hands the autistic man a wood block and a mallet and the band slides into a groove, nothing special, a groove like every other, a thousand bands in a thousand cities, everyone clapping on the two and four, someone singing over that, a thousand singers, but the sun through the cottonwoods, the smile blooming on the man's face, a woman dancing like a gypsy with her four-year-old girl, even the homeless men camped in the grass swept up in the beat, the groove, this clapping and tapping together in the now, this now where nothing bad has happened, where the bills aren't yet due, where the old wounds, where even the legless woman can dance, her arms all she needs now, the man on the stage laughing, looking out at the dancers—*he's making this happen all over the plaza*—music like rain, like rain, like steady rain after a long drought.

AFTER THE LOVELY OUTAGES

In the beginning it seemed our lives were a kind of bingo game
played in the dark, in alleys, on fire escapes, until the stapler
went missing, and you called and called—first letters and numbers
then numbers and numbers and finally letters and letters
to little effect. Our hair curled, then turned white, then
began to fall like the feathers from that swallow nest
you discovered in the vestibule after the water outage.
We knew it was late in the century when the museum's phones
gurgled and went out and the girl with the tattoo
of a waterfall on her shoulder was discovered wandering
among the Rembrandts, looking for the key to her mailbox.
You claimed the security guard's name was Nocona Burgess.
I still say it was Rhett Blackwood. His hair stood straight up
and he walked with a limp. But that was long ago, before the stars
lay down and spread their pale arms on the sidewalk
outside that house, the inside of which we'll never see again.

THE LIGHTED WORLD

The prison is built in a dark cave in the mountains. Every citizen, on his or her fiftieth birthday, is imprisoned for one year. It is the tradition. It is the law. Nobody remembers how it began. Nobody questions it.

For the individual prisoner the passing of time is marked only by a vague rumbling and howling, like the sound of a distant roller coaster, then a long silence, then a rumbling and howling again. The rumbling is the sound of a day in the outside world. Each silence is a night.

One of the prisoners marks her days by lining pebbles along the floor of her cell. When she has lined up seven small ones, she removes them and places a large white pebble in a different row, building a set of fifty-two. She now has fifty-one white pebbles lined up. As the howling begins again at the cave's mouth, she lines up her seventh smaller pebble. Her hands are shaking.

Her dreams, which are all she has had of a life, besides the small pleasures of eating and drinking when the person with the miner's light on his head clacks slowly through the cave and slips the food plate silently into her cell, have turned lately to nightmares. She has dreamed repeatedly of water rushing into the cave's mouth and sweeping through her cell. Last night she woke gasping for air. In the dream she was gripping the cell's bars as the water rose. She was pushing her face between the bars, trying desperately to gulp the last available air. She woke soaked with sweat, twisted in the blankets.

During the day, she has been thinking of her last days in the lighted world. Once dull, those memories have lately become vivid. But a strange thing has happened. Whereas once she would remember a series of images linked into a story, now the images float alone, wrenched out of any context, so she might see *her lover stand-ing alone at a train station, a light spring rain falling on his pale blue umbrella, then a red bird flashing across deep snow.* Or she'll hear *a coyote howling, a car starting, a group of people singing "Happy Birthday."*

This morning, she was shown *a lawn shimmering with silver frost, her mother brushing her hair before a vanity mirror, a great white bird lifting from the shore of a lake.* Each image was discrete, beauti-ful, but unrelated. *A rusty push mower abandoned in high grass. Underneath a shiny black car, a chestnut-colored moth the size of her hands, wings spread to reveal blue eyes. Her younger brother, three years old, standing alone at the end of a stranger's driveway, watching a red convertible pull slowly into traffic. Johnny-jump-ups, bright blue and yel-low flowers at the edge of a spring. The pale rose wash of light at sunrise on a farm. Two men leaning over a car hood, a map unscrolled there. A tractor dragging a harrow across freshly plowed earth. Redstarts flickering red and black overhead in the pale-green, budded branches of a swamp maple.*

For a week now, she has lain in her cell and watched the images, suddenly bright in the darkness. *Her sister stepping into a blue plastic pool, the water shimmering. A raccoon slinking across the dusky lawn. Tiny flying squirrels hurling themselves from the maple tree to the roof. Her father talking quietly; the car idling in the driveway with just the parking lights on. Smokey Robinson singing "Tears of a Clown" into a darkened room. The blue lights of a tape deck. Thump of a clutch pedal. A baseball ripping through branches and slapping into the web of her glove. She and her friends sliding a canoe into a river.*

As the howling outside the cave subsides, she drifts into sleep, the memory flashes fading into dream. This night, her last in the cave, she dreams of a great earthquake. Rocks are fracturing and breaking loose from the ceiling and walls, crashing around her. A large one slides down the wall, pinning her legs. She feels no pain, but she cannot move. She sees the flashing lights of rescue workers moving towards her, but she cannot speak. Men and women moan in pain in the darkness. Some kind of engine roars and rattles. She wakes. It's the sound of her last morning in the cave.

She rises from bed, rinses her face in the cold water that trickles off the cave wall.

A puppy gallops across a bright green lawn toward her, rocking from his back legs to his front, breathing fast, his tongue hanging from his mouth. A crisp day, bright green grass. Her father motions with his head and his hand—farther, farther—then tosses a football into the blue sky. A vulture rocks, hammocked in the wind above her head.

She can hear footsteps in the darkness. Four, maybe five, people are coming toward her cell. She can hear the ringing of keys. Now she can see the miner's lights flashing across stone.

A rock skittering across a flat lake at dawn. A careful boy printing his block letters on yellow paper at the desk in front of hers.

They are at her cell now. One shines a light on the lock, another slips the key in and unlocks the door.

A velvet green hummingbird hovering at a red columbine, its thin whiplike tongue lightly probing the blossom.

The iron door creaks open.

"Are you prisoner number 1835-C?" the man says, his deep voice booming in the near-silence of the cave.

Prisoner number 1835-C has not spoken for a year and when she does her voice surprises her with its softness: "Yes, I am."

"And are you ready to reenter?"

Her younger sister bouncing in the saddle of a pink plastic horse suspended on springs. Three boys swinging out on a tire, dropping twenty feet into a muddy river. A lizard twitching on a stucco wall.

"No?" she says, her body shaking with the effort, and then more certain: "No, sir, I am not."

"You understand that your refusal means it will be one full year before you will be eligible for release?"

"I do."

"Let it be noted that Prisoner 1835-C has refused reentry on January the first."

Someone makes a note in a ledger. The men don't understand the refusals, but it is not their job to understand or convince the prisoner, merely to record the date and the outcome. They each shake her hand, then leave, clanging the iron door shut behind them.

White cabbage moths fluttering over broccoli heads.

A horse standing alone in the rain.

A snake, a sleek gray racer with a yellow ring around its neck, pours itself like liquid down a ledge and disappears under a loose shard.

INSTRUCTIONS, MY TOWNSPEOPLE

The shadows of skyscrapers should have
Already cast a darkness. The sun

Should be a pale disk. Others
Should have waded bravely in. Should have

Fallen, that is, into the pit of, the loving
Arms of, the maw of. Take the tie.

The one that looks like something
Paul Klee painted on an off night.

Tie it neatly around my throat. Make me
Look like I have somewhere to go.

A little breeze, then, in my mouth
And hair. Lifelike, then, a smile.

Make me look back like I've got
A few quick errands to run—

Bank, cleaners—then drinks and dinner.
A wake-up call, an early flight. Make me

With my glass eyes look
Unrelenting in the eyes of the living.

Like I'm about to deliver a barb, a quip,
A goodbye disguised as a greeting.

ANTHEM

Cadillacs & catalexis. Burdens. Graces.

Jimi in the billowing, the blazon & hiss.

Black jeans, black boots. Lean as a stork.

Shades, circa Dylan '64.

Powder blue Strat lashed to his back.

Destiny wants him, wants pick slash,

shimmer & sweep, hammer-on,

elision & *crunk.* Wants hip thrust, amp hump,

tongue in the crease. The guitar's

lather & moan. Blue flames, dapple of headlights,

emergency whine & *blatt.* Long black fingers

on the maple neck. The banner, blood-spangled,

riven & shorn. *Home of the grave.* Then:

Blackout. Whipped free, that Strat,

in amplight & droning flung. Hazards, vexed

amplitudes, all of it, sputtering with avarice & shame.

EMPIRE

A sizeable hog
snoozing beside
the rusted abattoir.

Photograph by Jason S. Ordaz, Institute of American Indian Arts (IAIA), 2016

Jon Davis is the author of three previous full-length collections of poetry: *Preliminary Report*, *Scrimmage of Appetite*, and *Dangerous Amusements*. He is also the author of five limited-edition chapbooks and a limited-edition art book in collaboration with the artist Jamison Chas Banks, *Heteronymy: An Anthology*. *Dayplaces*, which Davis translated from the Arabic with the author, Iraqi poet Naseer Hassan, was recently published by Tebot Bach Press. Davis has received a Lannan Literary Award in Poetry, the Peter I.B. Lavan Prize from the Academy of American Poets, and two NEA Poetry Fellowships. He was Santa Fe's fourth Poet Laureate and directs the MFA in Creative Writing at the Institute of American Indian Arts, where he has taught since 1990.